Hard At Work, Andy Capp?

by
Smythe

A FAWCETT GOLD MEDAL BOOK

Fawcett Publications, Inc., Greenwich, Connecticut

HARD AT WORK, ANDY CAPP?

ANDY CAPP of the Daily Mirror, London

Published by special arrangement with Field Newspaper Syndicate

All inquiries should be addressed to Hall House, Inc.,
262 Mason Street, Greenwich, Connecticut.

ISBN 0-449-13725-2

Printed in the United States of America

10 9 8 7 6 5 4 3 2

LOOKIN' LIKE THAT?!

10-1-73

YOUR WISH IS MY COMMAND, O MASTER — WHAT WOULD YOU LIKE ME TO CHANGE INTO?

A WOMAN!!

Smythe

10-17-73

6-28

6-29

7-12

7-19

7-24

7-26

7-27

8-1

8-16

6-15

Other Fawcett Gold Medal Books
In the Andy Capp Series
by Smythe